Respect.

# PREQUELS

---

iINVENT Manuscript:
To wake up your ideas

---

Book Of Dhi Yoga:
Yoga to catch, plant and grow ideas in
our pursuits.
Ideas 1 to 108

---

# CONTENT

# THANK YOU

To the family I have
and the strangers I met along the way.
To each good experience
and the bad ones that led me a stray.
To my friends who were there when in
need and to those who showed me my
weak knees.
To the happy memories
and to the sad ones that made sure I don't
forget.
To the mother of all
and to the father I will meet one day.
I thank all of you for
the adventure of circles and the infinite
moments
in which we finally intersect.

Dec 7 2014  1.00 pm  @1816zenden

# ABOUT

Dhi is the essence within one which
resonates with ...
This resonance of ideas is
an effort to compliment one's unique
pursuit at work, school and home
with Dhi yoga to:
Balance in everything to catch
ideas. Open up to all to plant the
ideas.
Learn the lesson in each experience, be
it good or bad, to grow the ideas.
A good idea is one that helps us, others
and the environment.
If fish are special because they have fins
and birds are special because they have
wings, you and me, a human's strength is
the intellect to manifest ideas.

Oct 16th 2016  6 pm  @1816zenden

# A LETTER TO YOUR DHI

"As you embark on this journey called life,
remember, you do not have to
become anyone,
you were born a masterpiece,
you are the best and there is no one
else like you.
Taking one opportunity at a time
along the way,
whenever you give your best,
that best in you will be realized,
little by little.
And with each choice made,
you may face a resulting win or
loss,
good or bad,
yes or a no…

But, learning to share the lesson in
each experience
irrespective of the result,
will lead you to the best this life has to
offer. Wishing you give the best and learn
from the rest
as you embark on this journey called life."

May 22 2018 2pm  @1816zenden

IDEA:

Do all the ideas that come to us, good or bad, eventually lead us to the Truth?

May Dhi mind be filled with ideas
to balance.

May Dhi hearth be filled with love
to open up and bloom.

May Dhi breath be filled with
awareness to learn.

DHI-109
Feb 1 2017 3 pm @1816zenden

When the mind balances it will find
peace.
When the heart opens up it will find love.
When the breath becomes aware
then it will learn Dhi Truth.

DHI-110
Feb 1 2017 3 pm @1816zenden

# Is life an effort to manifest Truth?

DHI-111
Feb 1 2017 3 pm @1816zenden

Why we do what we do defines how we do it.

DHI-112
Feb 1 2017 3 pm @1816zenden

The only part that changes over time is
the "Why" factor.

DHI-113
Feb 1 2017 3 pm @1816zenden

When we anchor the mind onto the breath, Dhi Truth in each desire is realized.

DHI-114
Feb 1 2017 3 pm @1816zenden

The constant idea Dhi finally
comprehends in each conclusion
is Dhi Truth.

DHI-115
Feb 1 2017 3 pm @1816zenden

Whenever one gives the best, accepts what one gets and learns from the rest, meditation or innovation or ..

happens with each breath.

DHI-116
Feb 1 2017 3 pm @1816zenden

Just like an ocean carving a rock with each wave , Dhi keeps giving the best with each breath to manifest ideas in the space.

DHI-117
Feb 1 2017 3 pm @1816zenden

9 breaths a minute.

540 breaths an hour.

13000 breaths a day.

In other words,

13,000 opportunities to
learn to share the best each
day.

DHI-118
Feb 1 2017 3 pm @1816zenden

When we say what we think and do what
as we say, we experience Dhi Truth.

DHI-119
Feb 4 2017  8 pm @1816zenden

A father only wishes the kids become better than he is and don't make the same mistakes as he did. And in that effort of imparting values, sometimes without knowing makes the mistake of burdening the kids with one's own dreams.

DHI-120
Feb 4 2017  8 pm @1816zenden

A mother only wishes the kids to be safe, healthy and happy. And in the name of love, sometimes without knowing, makes the mistake of burdening the kids with one's own fears.

DHI-121
Feb 4 2017 8 pm @1816zenden

Dhi Friend:
Where two or more strangers connect
because they share the same idea(s) and
nothing else.

DHI-122
Feb 4 2017 8 pm @1816zenden

Dhi Family:
Where each one can be their own,
The worst in each other can be
expressed, No fear of any judgement,
Connected by the Truth.

DHI-123
Feb 4 2017 8 pm @1816zenden

In each moment the Truth within one manifests.

DHI-124
Feb 4 2017 8 pm @1816zenden

Who is the cause of happiness or pain
within me: You or Me or Dhi or ..

DHI-125
Feb 4 2017 8 pm @1816zenden

When one is true in ideas, speech and
action then Dhi finds true love.

DHI-126
Feb 4 2017 8 pm @1816zenden

Words, numbers and pictures are used
to paint Dhi's perspectives of the Truth.


DHI-127
Feb 7 2017 2 pm @1816zenden

In trying to make you love me , I found
the love within.

In trying to make you understand, I
understood me.

In trying to make you happy, I found
happiness within.

In trying to meet your expectations, I
realized the best in me.

In trying to show the way I found the
path.

In trying to find you within the crowd I
found you within me.

In trying to wish you the best, I found the blessing that was in hiding.

In the pursuit of love, I found the path to what seeks me.

In trying to be with you, I have become One within.

DHI-128
Feb 7 2017 2 pm @1816zenden

Greed, Lust, Desires: each time we say we don't want them, we get more of them.

But whenever we accept, acknowledge and become aware of them,

We get Dhi balance, open and learn.

DHI-129
Feb 7 2017 2 pm @1816zenden

The Truth in time never changes with time.

DHI-130
Feb 7 2017 2 pm @1816zenden

28

All that we claim to be ours,

Be it wealth, health or anything else,

It is all just a lease by design.

DHI-131
Feb 7 2017 2 pm @1816zenden

From Truth comes love,
From love comes peace,
From peace comes happiness:
with each breath that one takes.

DHI-132
Feb 7 2017 2 pm @1816zenden

The Truth is hidden behind love and peace
in each breath.

DHI-133
Feb 7 2017 2 pm @1816zenden

Learning is becoming aware of the Truth
in each result or experience or moment.

DHI-134
Feb 7 2017 2 pm @1816zenden

By giving the best and accepting whatever One gets,

The Truth may be witnessed in each breath.

DHI-135
Feb 7 2017 2 pm @1816zenden

Truth reflects onto the breath.
Breath reflects onto the heart.
The heart reflects onto the mind.
The mind reflects onto the body.

DHI-136
Feb 7 2017 2 pm @1816zenden

Mind over matter.
Heart over the mind.
Breath over the heart.
Truth over breath.

DHI-137
Feb 9 2017 1 pm @1816zenden

Some times living in the mind, Dhi make's choices per the desires.

And some times living in the heart, Dhi make's choices full of love.

Living in each breath, Dhi makes a choice out of awareness.

DHI-138
Feb 9 2017 2 pm @1816zenden

To be aware of the Truth in each
breath may be the purpose of Dhi.


DHI-139
Feb 9 2017 2 pm @1816zenden

Ego said to Dhi "I am right always.
Everything is mine. I am in control."

DHI-140
Feb 9 2017 2 pm @1816zenden

Being blind to the Truth cannot be fixed by opening up the eyes wider. But it may be cured by closing the eyes.

DHI-141
Feb 9 2017 2 pm @1816zenden

One who learns from each experience
and every one is a true student.

DHI-142
Feb 9 2017  2 pm  @1816zenden

Dhi hopes the mind will become best
friends with the breath so they may fall in
love someday.

DHI-143
Feb 12 2017  6 pm  @1816zenden

The mind, hearth and breath play for
Dhi's attention.

DHI-144
Feb 12 2017  6 pm  @1816zenden

## BALANCE

With balance do I center into the
Truth?

When one becomes aware in the breath,
Truth reflects.


DHI-145
Feb 18 2017  8 pm  @1816zenden

I sit here thinking about the mystery that
surrounds me only to realize the Truth
when I stop thinking.


DHI-146
Feb 18 2017  8 pm  @1816zenden

Awareness of the Truth in each breath is
be'ing.

DHI-147
Feb 21 2017  12 pm  @1816zenden

Where the mind meets the heart and the
heart meets the breath, there the Truth
will manifest.

DHI-148
Feb 21 2017  12 pm  @1816zenden

"I am" is what the mind said and
"We are" is what the heart said
to the silent breath.

DHI-149
Feb 21 2017  12 pm  @1816zenden

Life is a reflection of the Truth.

DHI-150
Feb 21 2017  12 pm  @1816zenden

Truth is universal though its
perceptions may be individual.

DHI-151
Feb 21 2017  12 pm  @1816zenden

In be'ing Truthful one resonates with the
universal Truth.


DHI-152
Feb 21 2017  12 pm  @1816zenden

Searching for the Truth leads one to the
far reaching boundaries of the universe
and the deep depths of the breath.

DHI-153
Feb 22 2017  1 pm  @1816zenden

Everything begins with the Truth.
Everything ends in the Truth.


DHI-154
Feb 24 2017  1 pm  @1816zenden

Each be'ing is a unique
resonance of the Truth.

DHI-155
Feb 24 2017  3 pm  @1816zenden

Witnessing the Truth manifest
into life with each breath is
be'ing.

DHI-156
Feb 24 2017  3 pm  @1816zenden

In awareness one resonates
with the Truth.

DHI-157
Feb 27 2017  9 pm  @1816zenden

Simplicity is discovered in the Truth.

DHI-158
Feb 27 2017  9 pm  @1816zenden

The Truth in life is hidden in
each breath.

DHI-159
Mar 2 2017  9 pm  @1816zenden

Dhi Path:
Peace to Love to Truth
or
Mind to Heart to Breath
per se.

DHI-160
Mar 2 2017  9 pm  @1816 zenden

Truth lives in you and me.
Life lives in the Truth.
All come to live in the breath.

DHI-161
Mar 2 2017  9 pm  @1816zenden

Mind finds peace,
The heart finds love,
And the breath finds awareness
in One Truth.

DHI-162
Mar 5 2017  9 pm  @1816zenden

Side track from the Truth with each
breath is the default setting of Dhi.. I
guess.

DHI-163
Mar 5 2017  9 pm  @1816zenden

Is Truth a deed or information or intelligence or existence of all of the above in one.

DHI-164
Mar 8 2017  9 pm  @1816zenden

Dhi may need courage to face the Truth.
But there is no set need to become aware
of the Truth.

DHI-165
Mar 9 2017  11 pm  @1816zenden

From the seed came the roots, stem,
leaves, the fruit.

And from all of them came the seed
which was hiding in the fruit.

DHI-166
Mar 10 2017  1 pm  @1816zenden

If Truth is within one and it is in all,
then where is it actually?

The Truth within one is in all. The Truth
in all is within one.

DHI-167
Mar 16 2017  9 pm  @1816zenden

The drop of ocean
became a wave,
Then it became the shore,
And it evaporated to become the cloud
in the hope of touching the sun a galore.
As it reached new highs,
It cooled to fall as a rain drop
into the puddle,
From which it flowed to the pond,
And into the river,
To finally merge again,
To become that drop in the ocean.

DHI-168
Mar 27 2017  9 pm  @1816zenden

## OPEN:

Being open in acceptance one may realize
the Truth, if Truth allows it to.

A baby in it's innocence is a reflection
of the Truth.

DHI-169
Mar 27 2017  9 pm  @1816zenden

When one experiences Truth, it is bliss.

DHI-170
Mar 29 2017  9 pm  @1816zenden

Wherever the truth goes,  peace and love
go.

DHI-171
Mar 29 2017  9 pm  @1816zenden

The foundation and the core of each
manifestation is the Truth.

DHI-172
Mar 29 2017  9 pm  @1816zenden

The Truth in one's intention is what
drives manifestation.

DHI-173
Apr 6 2017  2 pm  @1816zenden

Telling the Truth is the first experience of the Truth.

DHI-174
Apr 6 2017  2 pm  @1816zenden

When I look in the mirror, I feel young no
matter what the age.

Why?

A mirror always reflects the never aging
beautiful Truth within each one.

DHI-175
Apr 9 2017  5 pm  @1816zenden

Facts and figures are typically
utilized to try and communicate
Dhi perspective of the Truth.

DHI-176
Apr 11 2017  4 pm  @1816zenden

The path I lead is unique to me,
The path you lead is unique to you.
But the light that we shine to move
forward may help each other,
Provided we are going in Dhi same
direction towards Truth.

DHI-177
Apr 16  2017  10 pm  @1816zenden

Attention leads to Awareness.
Awareness leads to Witness.
Witness leads to the Truth.

DHI-178
Apr 16  2017  10 pm  @1816zenden

Truth plays hide and seek with the desire.

DHI-179
Apr 20  2017  3 pm  @1816zenden

There is always just One Truth.

DHI-180
Apr 23  2017  11 pm  @1816zenden

Truth reflects Truth.
Truth seeks Truth.
Truth merges with Truth.

DHI-181
Apr 23  2017  11 pm  @1816zenden

The scientists explore the universe
in search of Truth.
The philosophers dive deep in
meditation to comprehend
the Truth in this existence.

But the Truth is:
What ever one seeks has always
been right under the nose:
The breath.

DHI-182
Apr 23  2017  11 pm  @1816zenden

In each breath one may
comprehend the Truth within
evolving into love and the love
evolving into the different
colors, sounds, scents, tastes
and feel of this world.

DHI-183
Apr 23 2017  11 pm  @1816zenden

The mind contextualizes Truth,
The heart feels Truth,
The breath becomes aware of the Truth,
And Dhi comprehends the Truth
so one may witness all of the above.

DHI-184
Apr 23 2017  11 pm  @1816zenden

When the circle completes,
Truth emerges from the center.

DHI-185
May 2 2017  1 pm  @1816zenden

The underlying bond that holds each and
every relationship together is Truth.

DHI-186
May 2 2017  1pm  @1816zenden

The easiest is to speak Truth.

Next come the deeds driven by Truth.

Hard is comprehending Truth.

Toughest is to be resonating with the Truth.

DHI-187
May 5 2017  4 pm  @1816zenden

I thought this. You said that. They did
what? What happened?
Each one of the above
is a unique reflection of the Truth.


DHI-188
May 9 2017  7 am  @1816zenden

Dhi best within each be'ing is nothing but
the Truth.

DHI-189
May 11 2017  10 am  @1816zenden

Sometimes the mind may lie,

the heart may deceive.

But the breath is always aware of the Truth.

DHI-190
May 11 2017  10 am  @1816zenden

We are pre-programmed to pursue happiness

in the name of career, lifestyle and relationships.

But it is in the pursuit of Truth,

we meet happiness, love and peace right under our nose:

in the breath.

DHI-191
May 15 2017  2 pm  @1816zenden

Be it time, space or seasons and me,
Everything in this world changes
except for the Truth,
which remain ever itself
for eternity.

DHI-192
May 19 2017  1 pm  @1816zenden

LEARN:

Being humble and knowing we don't know anything about the Truth may lead Truth to bless us with Truth.

The only thing that is permanent in this
world is Truth.

DHI-193
May 19 2017  1 pm  @1816zenden

We make a choice with each breath.

When young it may be the desire to have something or being with someone or some place  that drives our choice.

A little bit into the adulthood one's choice may be driven by the intellect wanting the best this life has to offer.

As we mature, the choice may be driven by love or wanting to give the best one has.

And a day may dawn when one may witness Dhi Truth in each choice:

Is the choice being done in Awareness or Ignorance?

DHI-194
May 22 2017  12 pm  @1816zenden

Each breath is the gateway to the Truth.

DHI-195
May 24 2017  3 pm  @1816zenden

The mind makes a choice and so does the heart too. And to add to the confusion, the intellect makes one as well.

The question is not who made what choice, but was "I" aware or ignorant when the choice was made.

If one was aware, then the choice made by all the three will align Dhi with the Truth that put One in this position of making a choice in the first place.

DHI-196
May 24 2017  3 pm  @1816zenden

When two become one in love, an opportunity for Truth to take birth manifests.

DHI-197
May 27 2017  9 am  @1816zenden

In the breath all become one with the Truth.

DHI-198
May 27 2017  9 am  @1816zenden

When Truth befriends,
One becomes everyones friend.

DHI-199
Jun 2 2017   10 am   @1816zenden

When One says thank you to whatever come's on the way,

the path treaded will lead to Truth some day.

DHI-200
Jun 2 2017  10am  @1816zenden

The best within One is just plain old
Truth, Truth, Truth…

nothing but the Truth.

DHI-201
Jun 4 2017  1 am  @1816zenden

"I lie to my self all the time" thought I as
one took the first step towards the Truth.

DHI-202
Jun 6 2017  9 am  @1816zenden

An effort may be made to sense, explain
and understand the Truth.

But when all words fail and there is
nothing left to comprehend,

the Truth finally resonates.

DHI-203
Jun 10 2017  8 am  @1816zenden

Is everyone and everything just a
unique reflection of the same old
One Truth..

DHI-204
Jun 12 2017  11 am  @1816zenden

Is the journey to the Truth from
"inside out" or "outside in"?

I guess just depends on where One
is looking from?

DHI-205
Jun 14  2017  12 am  @1816zenden

To be or not to be with the Truth in each breath is a hope and a pursuit of the mind and the heart.

DHI-206
Jun 14  2017  12 am  @1816zenden

# Is manifestation an expression or impression of the Truth?

DHI-207
Jun 18  2017  9 am  @1816zenden

Dhi will run out of ink in trying to
describe the Truth.

DHI-208
Jun 18  2017  11 am  @1816zenden

Dear Mind.
Now that you know the Truth,
can we please live in Peace.

DHI-209
Jun 18 2017 11 am @1816zenden

Dear Heart.
Now that you know the Truth,
can we fall in Love.

DHI-210
Jun 20  2017  12 pm  @1816zenden

In each lie lies the Truth waiting to manifest.

DHI-211
Jun 20  2017  12 pm  @1816zenden

With each breath, one witnesses
awareness reflect in everything
around the self.

DHI-212
Jun 22  2017  2 pm  @1816zenden

From today is born tomorrow and
yesterday.

In Dhi breath all became one.

DHI-213
Jun 21 2017 1 pm @1816zendenn

114

Dhi is home when with Truth.

DHI-214
Jun 25  2017  9 pm  @1816zenden

Being Truthful to others is easy.
But being Truthful to one self is the challenge.

DHI-215
Jun 25  2017  9 pm  @1816zenden

Truth is reality.

DHI-216
Jun 25  2017  9 pm  @1816zenden

# DHI CREDITS

Everything in this book, be it the ideas, thoughts, concepts, stories, songs, perspectives and knowledge have been written, sung and communicated by many over the past centuries in their own context.

So what is emphasized in this effort is not original in any form or fashion except from the perspective of Dhi.

Hope we comprehend the words conveyed in their truest essence.

Respect.
Abhi DhiYogi

Oct 16th 2016  6 pm  @1816zenden

Book Of Dhi Truth By Abhi DhiYogi

NABROS & Partners LLC First Edition February 2024 Special discounts are available for education and in need institutes plus bulk orders.

An author event/concert may be requested.

For permission and all other requests please contact:

Publications @ NABROS & PARTNERS LLC. ,

4320 Winfield Rd: Suite 200, Warrenville, IL-60555, USA

i-INVENT.org | Email: hello@nabros.com |

Phone: +1 630 796 7676

Printed and created in the United States of America. Library of Congress Cataloging-in-Publication Data is available.

PRINT ISBN: 978-1-963651-02-7

EBOOK ISBN: 978-1-963651-03-4

www.ingramcontent.com/pod-product-compliance
Lightning Source LLC
Chambersburg PA
CBHW031242120626
46545CB00003B/1250